Mollie MAKES

CHRISTMAS

♡making ♡thrifting ♡collecting ♡crafting

CONTENTS

PUT YOUR OWN STAMP ON IT!

CUTE CHRISTMAS CHARACTERS

EMBROIDERED EMBELLISHMENTS

HOMEMADE DECORATIONS

DECK THE HALLS!

If you're hooked on crochet, hanker for handmade and would rather create your own unique Christmas than buy from a superstore, then this little book is for you. It perfectly captures the 'living and loving handmade' spirit of *Mollie Makes* magazine, celebrating the world of 'granny chic'.

Featuring over 20 new projects from *Mollie Makes* magazine's favourite designers, *Christmas* showcases a passion for handmade. Inspired in part by the huge online community of creative bloggers, the book reflects the cultural shift taking place towards rediscovering the crafting skills of previous generations. Now we too are recognising how satisfying it is for the soul to knit, crochet, fold, stitch and sew. From hand-crafted decorations for the home and Christmas table, to things to make and give as gifts, the book satisfies the growing desire to create something special.

Gretel Parker shares her needle felting skills and creates Christmas cottage tree trinkets – sure to become a treasured family heirloom to be packed away in tissue year after year. Another favourite is Cara Medus' fun Santa Kit – crocheted carrots, a mince pie and even a bottle of sherry!

Be thrifty and recycle unloved books into a star garland, or use pretty Japanese papers to make a miniature Christmas tree – perfect for small space living.

Did I mention Kirsty Neale's adorable felt finger puppets, or Carol Meldrum's knitted beaded baby bootees? Finally, if Santa has been very generous this year there's Charlie Moorby's chamois fawn felt appliqué iPad case. Way. Too. Cute.

All the projects are easy to follow with clear step-by-step photographs and instructions, plus handy tips along the way. Many are suitable for beginners, but the *Mollie Makes* ethos is to give it a go and be proud of the end result. We positively embrace imperfection.

Here's to Living and Loving a Handmade Christmas,

NEEDLE FELT
CHRISTMAS COTTAGES

SIMPLE NEEDLE FELTING IS THE PERFECT WAY TO CREATE A COSY COLLECTION
OF DECORATIONS FOR YOUR TREE. YOU CAN MAKE YOUR LITTLE HOUSES ANY SHAPE
YOU CHOOSE BY SCULPTING LOOSE WOOL ROVING WITH ONE OR TWO NEEDLES,
BUT LIMIT YOUR COLOURS FOR A STYLISH CO-ORDINATED LOOK.

CHRISTMAS
TREE
TRINKETS

HOW TO MAKE... CHRISTMAS COTTAGES

MATERIALS

SMALL AMOUNTS OF MERINO ROVING
IN SHADES OF RED, GREEN AND WHITE

ASSORTMENT OF HEART-SHAPED BUTTONS

SEED BEADS

SMALL JUMP RINGS AND SLIGHTLY LARGER
CURTAIN RINGS

EMBROIDERY THREADS TO MATCH
WOOL COLOURS

AT LEAST TWO SIZE 40 TRIANGULAR
FELTING NEEDLES AND HOLDER

A FELTING MAT (SPONGE OR BRUSH)

SEWING NEEDLE

TIP
To make variations on the basic cottage, simply roll or fold the wool into roughly the shape you want before modelling it with your needle. A small house like this should take 3–4 hours to make.

01 Take a length of 46cm (18in) roving teased out to a strip about 5cm (2in) wide. Fold the roving strip over and over to make a small oblong roll. This will form the base of the cottage.

02 With two needles in your holder, begin jabbing the wool using your non-needling hand to hold it in place. Needle felting is simply a form of modelling, so use your fingers and thumb as a guide to make the straight lines of the walls and corner angles. Work all sides equally to get a nice 3D shape.

03 After a while, you will feel the wool firming up and responding to the needle. Carry on working until you have a small, firm block measuring approx 4 x 2.5cm (1½ x 1in).

04 Now to make the roof. Take about 20cm (8in) of teased out red roving (see step 1) and place it centrally on top of the cottage base. Bunch up a plug of wool for a bit of extra filling inside and anchor it in with your needles.

05 Fold the edges over and towards the middle in a loose pyramid shape, and begin to shape a little roof, using your fingers and thumb to hold the wool in place. Don't forget to keep turning as you work so that your cottage looks great from all angles.

06 To get really precise edges, use one needle and a straight finger as a guide. Again using just one needle in your holder and working with tiny jabs, smooth and tidy the surface of your little house by needle felting thin layers of wool to cover the cottage walls and roof.

07 Now take a small amount of white roving and anchor a covering of snow to the roof. Outline the edge first in loose, natural waves, then fill it in. This is best done with one needle for a crisper finish.

08 Needle felt a little door onto the front of your house, and embroider and embellish as you choose. For example, sew on heart-shaped buttons for windows and seed beads to make the snow-covered roof glisten.

09 Finally, stitch a little jump ring into the top of the house, twist some matching embroidery threads into a cord, and thread them through. Tie the ends of the twisted cord to a small curtain ring ready for hanging.

TAKE CARE,
FELTING NEEDLES
ARE VERY SHARP!

GRETEL PARKER

Children's illustrator Gretel Parker
discovered needle felting four years
ago. Now her work is collected
all over the world and she enjoys
passing on her knowledge and
spreading the needle felting
'bug' to new crafters.
www.gretelparker.com

MIX AND MATCH

HEIRLOOM STOCKING

USE FESTIVE FABRICS, OR TEAM YOUR FAVOURITE FLORALS WITH BARGAIN VINTAGE FINDS. FINISH OFF WITH YOUR CHOICE OF RICRAC, RIBBONS, LACE AND DOILIES. HANG ABOVE THE FIREPLACE, AND — FINGERS-CROSSED — YOUR STOCKING WILL SOON BE FULL OF GORGEOUS GIFTS.

HOW TO MAKE... HEIRLOOM STOCKING

MATERIALS

FABRIC: APPROX 0.5M (½YD)
FOR EACH STOCKING

TRIMMINGS: RIBBONS, RICRAC, LACE,
BUTTONS, DOILIES

SCISSORS

SEWING MACHINE

SEWING NEEDLE

PINS

TIP
For an alternative design, cut a doily in half and shape the toe and heel using templates C and D as a guide. The yo yo flower can be replaced with a simple ribbon trimmed button.

01 Gather together your materials, choosing fabric and trimmings that complement each other. Photocopy the templates, scaling up as necessary, and cut out of paper. Fold your fabric neatly in half, and using template A cut out two stocking shapes from your main fabric.

02 Choose your lining fabric (if different) and cut out two more stocking shapes as in step 1. Using templates B, C and D, cut out one of each shape in your contrasting fabrics for your stocking top, toe and heel.

03 Press a 1cm (⅜in) hem at the bottom edge of the stocking top. Lay one main stocking piece flat, with right side facing you, and pin the stocking top in place. Machine stitch onto the stocking, and add any ribbons, lace or ricrac, pinning them in place before sewing on.

04 Next take your heel and toe pieces, pin in place, then sew onto the stocking. Use a zigzag stitch for added embellishment.

05 Take both main stocking pieces and pin right sides together. Machine stitch using a 1cm (⅜in) seam allowance, trim edges and snip into curves to allow for neat turning. Turn right way out and press over a 1.5cm (⅝in) hem around the top of the stocking.

06 Take the two lining pieces, pin and machine stitch right sides together with a 1cm (⅜in) seam allowance. Trim and snip seams (as step 5) but do not turn right way out. Press a 1.5cm hem (⅝in) along the top. Place the lining inside the main stocking.

07 Take a piece of ribbon approx 16cm (6¼in) long, fold in half and place the ends in between the main stocking and stocking lining; pin in place. Machine stitch a 6mm (¼in) hem around the top of the stocking and press.

08 To make the yo yo flower, cut a circle of fabric the size of a saucer and hand sew a running stitch along the edge all the way round. Draw up to gather the outside edge inwards and sew down in the centre.

09 Add a button to the centre and trim with ribbon. Sew the finished yo yo flower onto the stocking top.

SEE P95 FOR TEMPLATES

JANE HUGHES

Jane from littleteawagon is a crafter/designer with a fondness for 70's fabrics and wallpapers... making homewares and bags and blogging about a crafty life. www.teawagontales.blogspot.com

AMIGURUMI-STYLE
CROCHET REINDEER

THIS CHRISTMASSY CREATURE MAY OR MAY NOT BE RELATED TO SANTA'S FAVOURITE GIFT-DISTRIBUTING REINDEER, BUT HE CERTAINLY SHARES RUDOLPH'S GLOWING RED NOSE! MAKE HIM AS A STOCKING-FILLER PRESENT OR ADD HIM TO YOUR FESTIVE DÉCOR.

CUTE
CHRISTMAS
CHARACTER

HOW TO MAKE... CROCHET REINDEER

MATERIALS

100g BALLS (280m/306yd) OF HAYFIELD BONUS DK, ONE EACH IN OATMEAL 964 (A), ALPINE 842 (B) AND CHOCOLATE 947 (C), OR SIMILAR YARN (DK-WEIGHT ACRYLIC)

ODDMENTS OF RED AND WHITE DK YARN

SIZE 3mm (US C2/D3) & SIZE 3.5mm (US E4) CROCHET HOOKS

POLYESTER TOY STUFFING

POLYPROPYLENE GRANULES

TWO BLACK SEED BEADS FOR EYES

PIPE CLEANER

SEWING NEEDLE

PINS

TENSION TIP

Tension is not important for this project, as long as you make the crochet fabric nice and dense so the various items can be stuffed firmly and retain their shapes.

01 Make the body (starting at tail end). With yarn A and 3.5mm hook, make a magic loop, ch1, and work 6dc into the loop. Ss to the first ch to join.
Round 1: Ch1, 1dc into each st, ss to the first ch to join.
Round 2: Ch1, 2dc into each st, ss to the first ch to join. 12 sts
Round 3: Ch1, (2dc in the first st, 1dc) six times, ss to the first ch to join. 18 sts
Round 4: Ch1, (2dc in the first st, 2dc) six times, ss to the first ch to join. 24 sts
Round 5: Ch1, (2dc in the first st, 5dc) four times, ss to the first ch to join. 28 sts
Work another five rounds of 28dc.
Next round: Ch1, (dc2tog, 2dc) seven times, ss to the first ch to join. 21 sts
Next round: Ch1, 21dc, ss to the first ch to join.
Next round: Ch1, (dc2tog, 1dc) seven times, ss to the first ch to join. 14 sts
Next round: Ch1, 14dc, ss to the first ch to join.
Fill most of body with granules.
Next round: Ch1, (dc2tog) seven times, ss to the first ch to join. 7 sts
Next round: Ch1, 7dc to the first ch to join.

Fasten off, top up the stuffing using polypropylene granules and then sew up the hole.

02 Make the head.
With yarn A and 3.5mm hook, make a magic loop, ch1, and work 6dc into the loop. Ss to the first ch to join.
Round 1: Ch1, 2dc into each st, ss to the first ch to join. 12 sts
Round 2: Ch1, (2dc in the first st, 1dc) six times, ss to the first ch to join. 18 sts
Work another four rounds of 18dc.
Next round: Ch1, (2dc in the first st, 5dc) three times, ss to the first ch to join. 21 sts
Next round: Ch1, 21dc, ss to the first ch to join.
Next round: Ch1, (2dc in the first st, 2dc) seven times, ss to the first ch to join. 28 sts
Change to yarn B.
Next round: Ch1, 28dc, ss to the first ch to join.
Next round: Rep previous round.
Next round: Ch1, (dc2tog, 2dc) seven times, ss to the first ch to join. 21 sts
Next round: Ch1, (dc2tog, 1dc) seven times, ss to the first ch to join. 14 sts
Stuff with polyester toy stuffing.

Abbreviations

(UK terms used throughout)

beg: beginning

ch: chain

cont: continue

dc: double crochet

dc2tog: double crochet two stitches together (decrease by one stitch): insert the hook in the first st, yarn round hook and pull it through this stitch (2 loops on hook). Insert the hook into the second st, yarn round hook and pull it through this stitch (3 loops on hook). Yarn round hook and pull through all 3 loops on hook.

magic loop and ch 1: Make a loop with the yarn around your index finger so that there are two strands at the point where the ends pass one another. Put your hook underneath these two strands and pick up the yarn (make sure you use the working end which runs to the skein rather than the tail end), pulling it under the strands so that the yarn is over the hook. Pick up the yarn again and pull it through the loop on the hook to make one chain.

rep: repeat

ss: slip stitch

st(s): stitch(es)

UK/US crochet differences:

UK dc (double crochet) = US sc (single crochet)

01

02

TIP
When filling the body with poly-propylene granules, you might find it helpful to use a funnel made from a piece of paper to get them in – otherwise they may easily spill out.

Next round: Ch1, (dc2tog) seven times, ss to the first ch to join. 7 sts Fasten off, top up the stuffing using polyester toy stuffing and sew up hole, leaving a long tail of yarn to sew the head to the body.

03 Make four legs.
With yarn A and 3.5mm hook, make a magic loop, ch1, and work 6dc into the loop. Cont without closing off the round with a ss, so the next st to be worked will be the first of the 6dc. Cont working in a spiral in this fashion until the leg measures 4cm (1½in). Fasten off, leaving a long tail of yarn to sew the legs to the body. Fold a piece of pipe cleaner double so that it fits inside the length of the leg.

04 Sew the head on securely so that the top of the head is level with the top of the body. Make sure the seam of the head is turned towards the back, and that the seam of the body is underneath.

05 Make two ears.
With yarn A and 3.5mm hook, ch3 and join into a ring with a ss.
Row 1: Ch1, 3dc into ring, turn.
Row 2: Ch1, 1dc, 2dc in next st, 1dc, turn. 4 sts

Row 3: Ch1, (dc2tog) twice, turn. 2 sts
Row 4: Ch1, dc2tog. 1 st
Fasten off, leaving a tail of yarn to sew the ears to the head.
Pinch the base of each ear together and sew with a couple of stitches before attaching each ear to the top of the head.

06 Make the tail.
With yarn A and 3.5mm hook, ch5.
Row 1: Work 4dc beg with the second ch from the hook, ch1 and 4dc along the other side of foundation ch without turning. Ss into the point of the tail. Fasten off, leaving a long tail of yarn to sew the tail to the body. Sew in position just above the starting point of the body.

07 Sew the legs in position underneath the body.

08 Make two antlers.
With yarn C and 3mm hook, ch7. Leave a long tail of yarn at beg of the chain for sewing the antlers to the head.
Row 1: Work 6dc beg with the second ch from the hook, turn.
Row 2: Ss across 3 sts beg with the st at the base of the hook, ch7.

Row 3: Work 6dc beg with the second ch from the hook, ss into the first piece of 6dc to join, turn.
Row 4: Ss across 3 sts beg with the st at the base of the hook, ch4.
Row 5: Work 3dc beg with the second ch from the hook, ss into the second piece of 6dc to join, Fasten off.

09 Flip one antler over so that the antlers are symmetrical and sew to the top of the head.

10 Make the nose.
With red yarn and 3.5mm hook, make a magic loop and 6dc into loop. Ss to the first ch to join and fasten off, leaving a long tail of yarn to sew the nose to the head.

11 Add the finishing touches.
Sew the nose to the head. Mark the position of the eyes with two pins. Sew a few straight stitches with white yarn at these two points, and sew two black seed beads on top.

CARA MEDUS

Cara lives in Bristol with her husband and two boys. She loves designing things to knit and crochet, and occasionally finds some time to do a bit of illustration and papercraft. Her other passions are cake and coffee, preferably at the same time. www.caramedus.com

LINO-CUT
FESTIVE STATIONERY

IT'S EASIER THAN YOU THINK TO CREATE YOUR OWN LINO-CUT STAMP. YOU WILL
SOON BE PRINTING MATCHING CARDS, ENVELOPES, LABELS, WRAPPING PAPER AND
WHATEVER ELSE YOU CAN GET YOUR HANDS ON!

PUT YOUR OWN STAMP ON IT!

merry christmas

HOW TO MAKE... FESTIVE STATIONERY

MATERIALS

SPEEDY CARVE LINO BLOCK

LINO CUTTER AND BLADE

PENCIL

TRACING PAPER

SELECTION OF COLOURED CARD,
PAPER, GIFT TAGS AND ENVELOPES

INK PADS IN A SELECTION OF COLOURS

SCISSORS

TIP
Experiment with papers, colours and repeat printing to create patterns for your stationery.

01 Draw or trace a simple shape on a piece of tracing paper to create your stamp. Use the templates provided. Silhouettes work the best; think about what you would like to print and if you would like the image to be a positive or negative print.

02 Turn the tracing paper over and transfer trace your drawing onto your speedy carve lino block, making sure to leave space for cutting out around each. The pencil line should now be visible on your block.

03 Cut your designs out using scissors. Each will become a stamp.

04 Using the lino cutter very carefully cut away the lino around your design or inside your design depending on whether you would like to create a negative or positive print.

05 Now your lino stamp is complete, use your ink pads to ink it up and then press firmly onto your chosen paper, card or gift tag to create your print.

SEE P95 FOR TEMPLATES

ZEENA SHAH

Zeena Shah studied printed textile design at Chelsea School of Art & Design and has since worked in both the fashion and interiors textile industry. In late 2009, inspired by her love of paper cutting, printing, birds and hearts, she launched her own label, z e e n a – a collection of hand silk screen printed and handmade textiles for the home. Zeena also runs a programme of craft workshops, inspiring people to get stitching.
www.zeenashah.com

DOOR WREATH

GIVE THE WELCOMING DOOR WREATH, THAT TRADITIONAL FESTIVE DECORATION, A BRIGHT, MODERN LOOK. THE RUFFLES ARE EASILY MADE FROM FOLDED CIRCLES OF FELT PINNED IN PLACE ON A POLYSTYRENE BASE, AND THEN DECORATED WITH A MACHINE-STITCHED MISTLETOE EMBELLISHMENT. EASY TO MAKE RIBBON BOWS ADD A LUXURIOUS TOUCH.

EMBROIDERED
EMBELLISHMENTS

HOW TO MAKE... DOOR WREATH

MATERIALS

1.5M (1³/₄YD) OF 90CM (36IN) WIDE PURPLE FELT FOR THE WREATH

BRIGHT GREEN FELT MEASURING 25 x 25CM (10 x 10IN) PLUS SCRAPS OF WHITE FELT

GREEN SEWING MACHINE THREAD A SHADE DARKER THAN THE FELT

1M (1YD) OF 2CM (³/₄IN) WIDE SATIN RIBBON IN GREEN AND PURPLE

NARROW RIBBON, 8 CM (3¹/₈"), FOR HANGING

APPROX 175 DRESSMAKER'S PINS

25CM (10IN) POLYSTYRENE HALF-RING FORM

SCISSORS

WATER-ERASABLE FABRIC PEN

SEWING MACHINE

TIP
When fixing the ruffles to the polystyrene wreath you may want to use a thimble to press in the pins, especially as there are so many to attach!

01 Cut an 8cm (3⅛in) circle card template and use to mark approx 150 circles onto purple felt as close together as possible. Cut out.

02 To make a ruffle, take a felt circle, fold in half and crease to give you a semi-circle; fold in half again and put a pin through the point of the quarter circle.

03 To attach the felt ruffle to the wreath, push in the pin. Continue to fold and add more arranging them at different angles to enhance the ruffled effect, grouping them tightly so that the polystyrene cannot be seen.

04 To make the hanging loop, cut a 8cm (3⅛in) length of narrow ribbon. Fold in half and attach it to the back of the wreath with two or three pins.

05 Use the mistletoe template to cut nine sprigs from green felt. Cut out 36 small berries approx 6mm (¼in) in diameter from white felt.

06 Machine stitch the veins onto the sprigs. Start at the stem and stitch a row of small straight stitches down the centre and half way down the lowest leaf. Leaving the needle in the felt, raise the foot and rotate to stitch back up the leaf and up the stem. Continue to stitch veins down each leaf working your way back up to the top of the stem. As you stitch, the felt should curl slightly to create the mistletoe shape.

07 On each sprig, place a berry where each leaf meets the stem; machine stitch in place. Take three mistletoe sprigs and lay the stems on top of each other; machine stitch in place. Make two more sprig groups.

08 Use pins to attach the sprig groups to the lower half of the wreath in between the ruffles, making sure to press the pins in firmly.

09 To make a bow, take a 1m (1yd) length of ribbon and fold down one end by 10cm (4in). Continue to fold the ribbon in 10cm (4in) folds, one on top of the other. Machine a few small stitches at the centre to secure and insert two pins where you have stitched.

10 Fold the bow in half pulling all the loops up together, then carefully push it into the wreath in between the ruffles and close to where the mistletoe stems meet. Make and insert a second ribbon bow.

SEE P95 FOR TEMPLATES

HELEN NEWTON

Passionate about sewing and crafting, Helen loves to create beautiful, contemporary items using simple to learn techniques. Her aim is to inspire others to make something unique and original whilst having fun along the way.
www.lillyblossom.co.uk
www.etsy.com/lillyblossom

SIMPLE CROCHET
GRANNY SQUARE GARLAND

BRING A LITTLE FESTIVE FUN TO YOUR HOME WITH THIS VIBRANT CROCHET GARLAND.
THIS IS A GREAT STASH-BUSTING PROJECT AS EACH GRANNY SQUARE ONLY REQUIRES
A SMALL AMOUNT OF YARN, AND THE MORE COLOURS YOU USE, THE MORE LIVELY
THE EFFECT!

GREAT FOR
BEGINNERS

HOW TO MAKE... GRANNY SQUARE GARLAND

MATERIALS

DK YARNS IN YOUR CHOSEN COLOURS

SIZE 3.5mm (US E4) CROCHET HOOK

SCISSORS

DARNING NEEDLE

TENSION TIP
Tension is not important for this project, but using the same type of yarn for each square should ensure that all the squares end up the same size.

01 Make a slipknot in the end of the yarn and put the loop on to the crochet hook, then ch 4. Join with ss into first ch to form a ring.

02 **Round 1:** 3ch (counts as 1tr), 2tr into ring, 3ch, 3tr into ring, 3ch, *3tr into ring, 3ch, rep from * once more, ss into top of first ch.

03 **Round 2:** Ss across next 2tr to reach first corner ch sp, 3ch (counts as 1tr), 2tr into the first corner ch sp, 3ch, 3tr into the same ch sp (makes 1st corner), *3tr into next ch sp, 3ch, 3tr into same ch sp (makes 2nd corner); rep from * to make the 3rd and 4th corners, complete the round with ss into top of first ch.

04 **Round 3:** Ss across next 2tr to reach first corner ch sp, 3ch (counts as 1tr), 2tr into the first corner sp, 3ch, 3tr into same ch sp (makes 1st corner), *3tr into next ch sp (ch sp between the two sets of 3tr on the previous round), 3tr into second corner sp, 3ch, 3tr into same ch sp (makes 2nd corner); rep from * to make 3rd and 4th corners, 3tr into final ch sp, complete the round with ss into top of first ch.

05 **Round 4:** Ss across next 2tr to reach first corner ch sp, 3ch (counts as 1tr),

2tr into first corner sp, 3ch, 3tr into same ch sp (makes 1st corner), *3tr into next ch sp, 3tr into next ch sp, 3tr into second corner sp, 3ch, 3tr into same ch sp (makes 2nd corner); rep from * to complete the 3rd and 4th corners, 3tr into next ch sp, 3tr into final ch sp, complete the round with ss into top of first ch.

06 Cut yarn and weave in the loose yarn ends with the darning needle. Make 12 granny squares in all.

07 Join the squares together to make a garland. Choose a yarn colour for your chain to attach all the squares together and make 50ch to make the garland end.

08 Take your first square and ch into the top edge of the square to attach it, then ch into the top of every st along one edge of the square (should be approx 14 or 15ch for each edge to make sure the edge remains nice and square). Make 10ch for the length of garland between the first square and the next square.

09 Repeat step 8 until all 12 squares are attached, then make 50ch for the second garland end and tie off.

DESIGNED BY JANE HUGHES

Abbreviations

(UK terms used throughout)

ch: chain
ch sp: chain space
rep: repeat
ss: slip stitch
tr: treble
UK/US crochet differences:
UK tr (treble) = US dc (double crochet)

FESTIVE IDEAS

TRIM
THE TREE

01

A pretty paper and clothes peg angel design from Kirsty Neale that can be used to clip up Christmas cards, decorate your tree or as a cute alternative to a bow, holding gift tags in place.
www.kirstyneale.typepad.com

02

These sweet decorations from Eva Gáti are so simple to make – roll your paper into a cone, trim the excess at the top, edge with lace ribbon and add a handle. Make 24 for a Christmas tree advent calendar. For more great ideas from Eva visit her blog kiflieslevendula.blogspot.com

03

Let Annabelle Ozanne's 'Lil branch of glee...' inspire you to transform a tree branch into a Christmas display, adorned with handmade paper and crochet decorations and thrifty sales purchases.
threeredapples.blogspot.co.uk

DECK THE WALLS

04

This little wooden Christmas tree by Ingrid Jansen of Wood & Wool Stool is handmade from recycled pieces of wood with small hooks screwed in to add decorations. A small piece of string is attached to the back so it can be hung on the wall. For more designs see www.woodwoolstool.com

05

If you make your own stocking it can be as large as you like! This design from Charlotte Lyons is made using her Walnut Hill Farm range of patterned material and you can have fun embroidering the details in the fabric. www.blendfabrics.com

06

This bunting-style advent calendar from Jooles Hill, and made from Tilda fabrics, will help you to count down the crafty days to Christmas. For lots more festive ideas visit Joole's blog sewsweetviolet.blogspot.co.uk

SCANDINAVIAN-STYLE
PAPER CUT ORNAMENT

THIS PAIR OF PAPER CUT DECORATIONS ARE BASED ON THE WOODEN DALA HORSES OF SWEDEN. ORIGINALLY MADE AS TOYS FOR CHILDREN, THEY WERE CARVED IN THE LONG, DARK WINTER EVENINGS, THEN PAINTED IN BRIGHTLY COLOURED PATTERNS. MAKE YOURS IN RED AND WHITE, THE TRADITIONAL CHRISTMAS COLOURS OF SCANDINAVIA.

MAKE A MATCHING PAIR

HOW TO MAKE... PAPER CUT ORNAMENT

MATERIALS

TWO SHEETS OF WHITE A4 (US LETTER) PAPER

TWO SHEETS OF RED A4 (US LETTER) CARD

TRACING PAPER

H AND 2H PENCILS

GLUE

SMALL PAIR OF SHARP, POINTED SCISSORS

CRAFT KNIFE AND RULER

TIP

For a pretty garland, mount a number of paper cut horses on different coloured card and attach to lengths of ribbon. Or make miniature versions as place cards for the Christmas table.

01 Use a soft H pencil to trace off the horse design from the template. Turn the tracing paper over, lay it down on a sheet of white paper and use the harder 2H pencil to go over the inner outline of the horse and the marked patterns.

02 Cut out the shape and following the fold lines on the template, fold the horse in half and half again, making sure that the centre panel design is on the outside of the fold (see photo).

03 Use a small pair of sharp, pointed scissors to cut away the design.

04 Open up the horse and fold over the tail section along the fold line marked on the template; cut out the triangle pattern and open out. Repeat for cutting the patterns first on the legs, then the neck, and finally the eye section.

05 Transfer the outer outline of the horse onto some red card and cut out.

06 Cut out two stands from red card and score down the edge of each 1cm (⅜in) in from the side, following the line marked on the template and using a craft knife to just break the surface. Crease the scored lines to form glue flaps.

07 Glue the white paper cut to the red card – pencil marks facing down – making sure that you have a border of red card all around. If you are using a glue stick, take care on the delicate cut section as it can tear. Alternatively, you could use an adhesive spray: work in a well-ventilated area and follow the manufacturer's instructions.

08 Glue the stands to the back of the horse, lining up the base with the bottom edge of the legs.

09 Repeat steps 1–8 to make another horse, but this time turn the trace over so that the horse faces the other way.

SEE P93 FOR TEMPLATES

CLARE YOUNGS

Designer-maker Clare was given a craft book with a pile of paper and fabric at the age of eight and she hasn't stopped making since! Having trained as a graphic designer, she worked in packaging and illustration until turning to craft full time five years ago. Clare has written several craft books – to find out more visit www.clare@youngs-studio.com

HAND-EMBROIDERED
BAUBLE GIFT BAGS

SEW UP THESE LITTLE BAGS TO ADD A HANDMADE TOUCH TO SMALL GIFTS AND FESTIVE TREATS. AT JUST 9CM (3½IN) WIDE AND 16.5CM (6½IN) HIGH (INCLUDING HANDLES), THEY ARE SMALL ENOUGH TO HANG FROM THE TREE. THE HARDEST PART OF THIS PROJECT IS CHOOSING WHICH OF THE FIVE SMILING ORNAMENT MOTIFS TO EMBROIDER!

IDEAL
FOR TREE
PRESENTS

HOW TO MAKE... BAUBLE GIFT BAGS

SEE P94 FOR TEMPLATES

MATERIALS: PER GIFT BAG

ONE PIECE OF LIGHT-COLOURED COTTON FABRIC MEASURING 13 x 13CM (5 x 5IN)

EMBROIDERY THREADS: SILVER GREY, BLACK, AND BRIGHT CHRISTMAS COLOURS

ONE PIECE OF BRIGHTLY-COLOURED FELT MEASURING 10 x 30CM (4 x 12IN) FOR BAG

TWO PIECES OF CONTRASTING FELT MEASURING 1 x 15CM (⅜ x 6IN) FOR HANDLES

WATER-ERASABLE FABRIC PEN

EMBROIDERY HOOP AND EMBROIDERY NEEDLE

SCISSORS, PINS AND IRON

TIP

Made from felt, these little bags are perfect for lightweight gifts, but if you do plan to place something a little heavier in the bag, double the handles so they don't stretch.

01 Trace your chosen motif onto the light-coloured fabric. Place the fabric in the embroidery hoop to keep it nice and taut as you stitch.

02 Embroider your chosen motif. Use six strands of thread and stem stitch for the ornament outline, and three strands for everything else. Use backstitch (see p87) for the ornament details, French knots (see p87) for the eyes and an open detached chain for the mouth.

03 Remove the embroidered fabric from the hoop and trim to 7 x 9cm (2¾ x 3½in).

04 Fold the bag felt in half. Place the gift bag template on the fold, pin in place and trim around the sides and top edge. Cut out the opening on one side only.

05 Pin the embroidered panel into the opening; use running stitch (see p87) and three strands to sew in place.

06 Stitch each handle in place inside the scalloped edge using a simple cross stitch and three strands.

07 Fold the bag in half, right sides facing; press. Keeping the crease together, fold the bag back on itself, wrong sides facing, and make a 1.3cm (½in) gusset each side of the fold. Pin in place.

08 Stitch the sides of the bag with running stitch and three strands.

09 Make more bags using different motifs – there are five to choose.

MOLLIE JOHANSON

Mollie Johanson began her blog Wild Olive as a creative outlet. Dreaming and doodling have resulted in embroidery and paper projects, most featuring simply expressive faces. Mollie lives near Chicago, commuting daily to her in-home studio via the coffee pot. www.wildolive.blogspot.co.uk

Stem stitch

Detached chain

FELT APPLIQUÉ
IPAD COSY

DRESS UP YOUR FAVOURITE GADGET FOR THE HOLIDAY SEASON WITH THIS SUPER SNUG COSY FEATURING A GREAT LITTLE RETRO DEER MOTIF. FELT IS ONE OF THE EASIEST MATERIALS TO WORK WITH AND THIS SIMPLE DESIGN CAN BE COMPLETELY STITCHED BY HAND — NO SEWING MACHINE REQUIRED!

HOW TO MAKE... IPAD COSY

MATERIALS

TWO PIECES OF BABY BLUE FELT
MEASURING 33 x 21CM (13 x 8¼IN)

ONE PIECE EACH OF RED AND BEIGE FELT
MEASURING 20 x 13CM (8 x 5IN)

SCRAPS OF BABY BLUE, MEDIUM BROWN,
DARK BROWN, PINK AND WHITE FELT
FOR ACCENTS

EMBROIDERY THREAD: RED, BLUE, BEIGE,
WHITE AND BLACK

SIX SMALL OPAQUE SEED BEADS

SMALL PAIR OF SHARP, POINTED SCISSORS

FABRIC GLUE

SHARP SEWING NEEDLE

TIP
Don't have an iPad? No worries!
Just reduce the template sizes
to fit your favourite gadget, or
make it into a hot water bottle
cover instead.

01 Use the templates to cut out the following pieces from your felt fabric: a red oval, beige deer, medium brown ear details, white eye, blue collar and three pink baubles. You will also need a small circle of dark brown felt for the deer's pupil and a slightly larger circle of dark brown felt for his nose.

02 Take one of your baby blue felt rectangles and pin the red felt oval onto it 5cm (2in) from the bottom. Hand sew securely in place with small neat running stitches, using a sharp needle and a single strand of red embroidery thread.

03 Pin the deer motif on top of the red oval and hand stitch in place, again with running stitch, using a single strand of beige embroidery thread to match your felt colour.

04 Glue or stitch on the smaller felt accents using the photograph on p43 as your guide. When you are happy that all the felt layers are securely in place, use a sharp needle and single strand of black embroidery thread to add the eyelashes to the eye and long stitches to the hanging baubles.

05 To finish the embellishment of the front of the iPad cosy, add a few freehand snowflakes in opposite corners of the design using a single strand of white embroidery thread and the opaque seed beads. Our design has a total of six, but you can add as many as you like for a more festive finish.

06 Before stitching together the back and front pieces of your iPad cosy, you need to strengthen the top edges of the felt. Simply fold over the top edge of each piece by 5cm (2in) towards the right side of the fabric. Using blue embroidery thread, secure each flap by stitching down the sides and along the bottom edge with a neat running stitch.

07 Align the front and the back pieces of your iPad cosy, wrong sides together, and pin in place. With the deer motif facing you, blanket stitch all the way around the edges using all six strands of blue embroidery thread to match.

SEE P95 FOR TEMPLATES

CHARLIE MOORBY
aka THE SAVVY CRAFTER

Charlie is a thrifty craft blogger and incurable stitching addict with a penchant for anything handmade. Commissioning Editor by day and crafter by night you'll find her collecting buttons and hoarding ribbons on a daily basis.
She's a dab hand with a pencil and loves a spot of cross stitching too.
Find her online at
thesavvycrafter.blogspot.co.uk

KNIT WITH BEADS

BABY BOOTEES

ADD A TOUCH OF SPARKLE TO BABY'S FIRST CHRISTMAS WITH THESE CUTE BEADED BOOTEES. WITH A CLASSIC T-BAR BUTTON STRAP, THEY FIT SNUGLY AND SECURELY AROUND BABY'S FEET. THE INSTRUCTIONS PROVIDED ARE FOR THE CREAM BOOTEES WITH RED SOLES BUT, AS YOU CAN SEE, YOU CAN EASILY CHANGE THE COLOUR OF THE YARN AND BEADS.

FOR BABY'S
FIRST
CHRISTMAS

HOW TO MAKE... BABY BOOTEES

MATERIALS: CREAM BOOTEES

50G BALLS (80M/93YD) OF ROWAN HANDKNIT COTTON, ONE EACH IN ECRU 251 (A) AND ROSSO 215 (B), OR SIMILAR YARN (DK-WEIGHT COTTON)

ONE PAIR OF 3.25MM (US 3) KNITTING NEEDLES

DEBBIE ABRAHAMS BEADS SIZE 6/0: ONE PACKET OF CLEAR BEADS

SHARP SEWING NEEDLE AND FINE SEWING THREAD TO STRING THE BEADS ONTO YARN

TAPESTRY NEEDLE

TWO SMALL SHELL BUTTONS

TENSION TIP

25 sts and 32 rows to 10cm (4in) square over st st using 3.25mm needles. Finished size approx 9cm (3½in) long; width at toe approx 4.5cm (1¾in).

01 Thread the beads onto your main colour yarn (yarn A) before you start the pattern. You will need about 76 beads per bootee, but it is best to string more beads than are required than too few. Take a 10cm (4in) length of sewing cotton and thread a sharp sewing needle with it. Tie a knot at the end to form a loop. Place the end of the yarn through the sewing thread loop and press the fold of yarn with your finger and thumb to flatten slightly; this will help the beads to slide on more easily. Next, pick up a bead with the sewing needle, slip the bead down the needle and thread, and then slip it down onto the yarn. Repeat this process until all 76 beads have been threaded onto the yarn.

02 Knit the cream bootees (make 2 the same).
Start with the sole:
Using yarn B and 3.25mm needles, cast on 30 sts.
Row 1: K1, yfwd, k13, yfwd, k1, yfwd, k1, yfwd, k13, yfwd, k1. 35 sts
Row 2: K1, ktbl, k13, ktbl, k1, ktbl, k1, ktbl, k13, ktbl, k1.
Row 3: K2, yfwd, k13, yfwd, k2, yfwd, k3, yfwd, k13, yfwd, k2. 40 sts

01

CAROL MELDRUM

Carol is a textile designer, author and workshop tutor based in Glasgow who enjoys nothing better than playing around with yarn, coming up with new ideas and sharing them with folk at www.beatknit.com and blog.beatknit.com

Row 4: K2, ktbl, k13, ktbl, k3, ktbl, k2, ktbl, k13, ktbl, k2.
Row 5: K3, yfwd, k13, yfwd, k4, yfwd, k4, yfwd, k13, yfwd, k3.
45 sts
Row 6: K3, ktbl, k13, ktbl, k4, ktbl, k4, ktbl, k13, ktbl, k3.
Break off yarn B.
Join in yarn A.

03 Place beads.
Row 1: K1, *B1, k1, rep from * to end.
Row 2: Purl to end.
Row 3: K2, *B1, k1, rep from * to last st, k1.
Row 4: Purl to end.
Start to shape toe on next row, keeping bead pattern correct.
Row 5: K1, *B1, k1, rep from * until 26 sts have been worked, k2togtbl, turn.
Next row: Sl1, p7, p2tog, turn.
Next row: Sl1, k1, (B1, k1) 3 times, k2togtbl, turn.
Next row: Sl1, p7, p2tog, turn.
Next row: Sl1, (B1, k1) 3 times, B1, k2togtbl, turn.
Next row: Sl1, p7, p2tog, turn.
Next row: Sl1, k1, (B1, k1) 3 times, k2togtbl, turn.
Next row: Sl1, p7, p2tog, turn.
37 sts
Next row: Sl1, k1, *B1, k1, rep from * to end.
Next row: Purl to end.

04 Make top and T-bar.
Now work 3 rows in purl, ending with a RS row.
Cast off 17 sts knitwise, k2 (3 sts on RHN for vertical part of T-bar), cast off knitwise to end.
Break off yarn.
With RS facing, slip the knitting needle out of the 3 sts and insert back into position as if to work a knit row.
Rejoin yarn and work in garter stitch for 18 rows. Cast off knitwise.

05 Complete strap for left bootee.
With RS facing, and the toe of the bootee to the right, count along 16 sts from the back open edge, insert needle and pick up 3 sts, turn and work 16 rows in garter stitch.
Make buttonhole as follows:
K1, yfwd, k2togtbl, turn, work a further 2 rows in knit, k3tog, break off yarn.

06 Complete strap for right bootee.
With RS facing, and the toe of the bootee to the left, count along 13 sts from the back open edge, insert needle and pick up 3 sts, turn and work 16 rows in garter stitch.
Make buttonhole as follows:
K1, yfwd, k2togtbl, turn, work a further 2 rows in knit, k3tog, break off yarn.

07 To finish off, sew in all the loose ends, then gently press the toe and sides on the WS of the bootee. Using mattress stitch, sew up the back seam and sole of the bootee.

To complete the strap, fold over the vertical strap at the front of the bootee towards the inside and sew together to form a loop approx 2cm (¾in) for the horizontal strap to fit through. Slip the horizontal strap through the loop, then sew a button onto the side of the bootee to match up with the buttonhole.

Abbreviations

(UK terms used throughout)
B1: Bead 1 as follows: bring bead up to back of knitting, bring yarn forward to the front of work between needles, make sure bead is sitting at the front of work, slip the next stitch purlwise, then bring the yarn between the needles to the back of the work, wrapping the slipped stitch and making sure the bead is sitting to the front.
k: knit
k2togtbl: knit two stitches together through the back loop
k3tog: knit three stitches together
ktbl: knit through the back loop
p: purl
p2tog: purl two stitches together
rep: repeat
RHN: right-hand needle
RS: right side
sl1: slip one stitch
st(s): stitch(es)
WS: wrong side
yfwd: yarn forward

CROCHET TRADITIONS
SANTA KIT

SANTA HAS TO WORK HARD AT CHRISTMAS TIME, SO IT'S ONLY GOOD MANNERS
TO LEAVE HIM A LITTLE SOMETHING TO SAY THANK YOU. MAKE A BOTTLE AND
A MINCE PIE TO LEAVE BY THE FIRESIDE, AND DON'T FORGET TO MAKE CARROTS
FOR HIS FAITHFUL REINDEER...

HOW TO MAKE... SANTA KIT

DESIGNED BY CARA MEDUS

MATERIALS: MINCE PIE

100g BALLS (280m/306yd) OF HAYFIELD BONUS DK, ONE EACH IN ALPINE 842 (A) AND CHOCOLATE 947 (B), OR SIMILAR YARN (DK-WEIGHT ACRYLIC)

25g BALLS (70m/77yd) OF HAYFIELD BONUS TOYTIME DK, ONE EACH IN WHITE 961 (C), SIGNAL RED 977 (D) AND EMERALD 916 (E), OR SIMILAR YARN (DK-WEIGHT ACRYLIC)

SIZE 3mm (US C2/D3) & SIZE 3.5mm (US E4) CROCHET HOOKS

POLYESTER TOY STUFFING

CARDBOARD

GLUE

SEWING NEEDLE

TENSION TIP
Tension is not important for this project, as long as you make the crochet fabric nice and dense so the various items can be stuffed firmly and retain their shapes.

HOW TO MAKE...THE MINCE PIE

01 Make the pie base.
Using 3.5mm hook and yarn A, make a magic loop, ch1 and 6dc into the loop. Ss to the first ch to join before pulling up the loop.
Round 1: Ch1, 2dc in each dc of the previous round, ss to the first ch to join. 12 sts
Round 2: Ch1, (2dc in next st, 1dc) six times, ss to the first ch to join. 18 sts
Round 3: Ch1, (2dc in next st, 2dc) six times, ss to the first ch to join. 24 sts
Round 4: Ch1, (2dc in next st, 3dc) six times, ss to the first ch to join. 30 sts
Round 5: Ch1, (2dc in next st, 4dc) six times, ss to the first ch to join. 36 sts
Round 6: Ch1, 36dc worked in the back loop only, ss to the first ch to join.
Work another three rounds of 36dc, working through both loops as normal.

02 Make the picot edging.
Next round: Ch1, *dc in next st, ch2, ss in the first of those ch2, dc in next st **. Rep from * to ** until every st in the round is worked, then ss to the first ch to join.
Fasten off.

03 Make the mincemeat topping.
Using 3.5mm hook and yarn B, make a magic loop, ch1 and 6dc into the loop. Ss to the first ch to join before pulling up the loop.
Work rounds 1–5 as for Pie Base.
Work another round of 36dc.
Fasten off.

04 Make the icing.
Using 3mm hook and yarn C, make a magic loop, ch1 and 6dc into the loop. Ss to the first ch to join before pulling up the loop.
Work rounds 1–3 as for Pie Base.
Next row: Ch1, 3dc, turn.
Next row: Ch1, dc2tog, 1dc, turn. 2 sts
Next row: Ch1, dc2tog. 1 st
Ss down the side of these short rows towards the original round, finishing with a ss in the st on the end of the first short row. Ss over the next 2 sts
Next row: Ch1, 6dc, turn.
Next row: Ch1, dc2tog, 2dc, dc2tog, turn. 4 sts
Next row: Ch1, 1dc, dc2tog, 1dc, turn. 3 sts
Next row: Ch1, dc2tog, 1dc, turn. 2 sts
Next round: Ch1, dc2tog. 1 st
Ss down the side of these short rows

FOR PATTERN ABBREVIATIONS SEE P57

towards the original round, finishing with a ss in the st on the end of the first short row. Ss over the next 3 sts.

Next row: Ch1, 4dc, turn.

Next row: Ch1, (dc2tog) twice, turn. 2 sts

Next row: Ch1, dc2tog. 1 st

Ss down the side of these short rows towards the original round, finishing with a ss in the st on the end of the first short row. Ss over the next 2 sts.

Next row: Ch1, 2dc, turn.

Next row: Ch1, 2dc, turn.

Next row: Ch1, dc2tog. 1 st

Ss down the side of these short rows towards the original round, finishing with a ss in the st on the end of the first short row.

Ss over each remaining st to complete the round and ss to the first ch to join. Fasten off.

05 Make two holly berries.
Using 3mm hook and yarn D, make a magic loop, ch1 and 6dc into the loop. Ss to the first ch to join before pulling up the loop. Fasten off, leaving a long tail of yarn to sew the 6dc together into a small ball. Use the other end of the yarn (from the magic loop) to stuff the berry before sewing up.

06 Make two holly leaves.
Using 3mm hook and yarn E, ch6. Skip ch at base of hook and ss in the next ch.
Ch1, *dc in next, ch3, ss in the first of those ch, dc in next st. **
Rep from * to **.
Ch2 and ss in the other side of the dc just worked.
Cont working down other side of foundation ch.
Rep from * to ** twice, ss in the point of the leaf. Fasten off.

07 Make up the mince pie.
Weave in all loose ends. Cut a circular piece of cardboard to fit inside the bottom of the pie base and glue in place.

08 Sew the mincemeat topping to the pie base just below the picot edging. Sew nearly all the way round and stuff with polyester toy stuffing before completing the round of sewing.

09 Sew the icing, holly and berries on top of the mince pie.

MATERIALS: BOTTLE

100G BALLS (280M/306YD) OF HAYFIELD BONUS DK, ONE EACH IN CLARET 841 (F) AND ALPINE 842 (A), OR SIMILAR YARN (DK-WEIGHT ACRYLIC)

25G BALLS (70M/77YD) OF HAYFIELD BONUS TOYTIME DK, ONE EACH IN WHITE 961 (C), SIGNAL RED 977 (D) AND BLACK 965 (G), OR SIMILAR YARN (DK-WEIGHT ACRYLIC)

SIZE 3MM (US C2/D3) & SIZE 3.5MM (US E4) CROCHET HOOKS

CARDBOARD

GLUE

OLD PAIR OF TIGHTS OR SOCK

POLYPROPYLENE GRANULES

POLYESTER TOY STUFFING

TWO BLACK SEED BEADS FOR EYES

GOLD LUREX THREAD

SEWING NEEDLE

THREAD MARKER

HOW TO MAKE...THE BOTTLE

01 Make the bottle.
Using 3.5mm hook and yarn F, make a magic loop, ch1 and 6dc into the loop. Leave a long tail of yarn from the magic loop (approx 30cm/12in). Ss to the first ch to join before pulling up the loop.
Work rounds 1–6 as for the Pie Base. Cont to work rounds of 36dc (through both loops of the dc), working in a spiral without closing off the round with a ss, until the bottle measures 9cm (3½in) high.

02 Weight and stuff the bottle.
Cut a circular piece of cardboard to fit inside the bottom of the bottle. Pierce a hole in the centre of the card, and thread the tail of yarn from the magic loop onto a needle and pass it through the hole in the card. Glue the underside of the card to the base of the bottle, and leave the tail of yarn with needle attached. Take the foot from an old pair of tights or an old sock, and fill it with polypropylene granules so that it makes a small ball that will fit inside the bottle. Tie or sew together the end of the tights/sock, and using the tail of yarn and needle, pass the needle up through the ball and back down again, through the hole in the piece of card and secure the end to the base of the bottle.

03 Continue working on the bottle.
Place a short piece of thread (use a contrasting colour so it is easy to see) between the stitches to mark the beginning of the round, and continue to work in a spiral without closing off the round with a ss.
Next round: (1dc, dc2tog) twelve times to end of round. 24 sts
Move thread marker up one row after the end of each round.
Next round: (2 dc, dc2tog) six times to end of round. 18 sts
Next round: (7 dc, dc2tog) twice to the end of round. 16 sts
Next round: (6dc, dc2tog) twice to the end of round. 14 sts
Stuff the bottom portion of the bottle firmly using polyester toy stuffing. You can remove the thread marker.
Cont working in a spiral of dc on these 14 sts until the bottle neck measures 5cm (2in) high.
Change to yarn G, ss into the next st, ch1, and cont with three rounds of 14dc in black. Ss to the next st. Stuff neck of bottle using polyester toy stuffing.

Next round: Ch1, (dc2tog) seven times, working in the back loop of the dc only. 7 sts
Ss to the first ch to join, fasten off and sew up hole.

04 Make the label.
With 3.5mm hook and yarn A, ch13, turn.
Row 1: Work 12 dc beg in second ch from hook, turn.
Cont to work another thirteen rows of dc, then fasten off.

05 Make Santa's beard and hair.
With 3mm hook and yarn C, ch10, turn.
Row 1: Beg in second ch from hook, 2 ss, ch1, 1dc in next ch, ch3, skip 3ch, dc in next ch, turn.
Row 2: Ch1, dc2tog (insert hook into ch sp for 2nd of these), 1dc into ch sp, dc2tog (insert hook into ch sp for first of these), turn.
Row 3: Ch1, 3dc, 2 ss down side of beard and 2 ss in the remaining ch at the end of beard.
Ch10 (to make a line of 'hair' that will be sewn along the bottom edge of the hat) and ss to the other side of the beard to join.
Fasten off.

06 Make Santa's hat.
With 3mm hook and yarn D, ch7.
Row 1: Make 6 dc beg in second ch from hook, turn.
Row 2: Ch1, dc2tog, 4dc, turn. 5 sts
Row 3: Ch1, 3dc, dc2tog, turn. 4 sts
Row 4: Skip st at base of hook and 3 ss.
Ss 1 in the end of each row to carry yarn to the bottom of the hat.
Ch4, skip first ch and 3 ss back along ch. Ss to corner of hat to join.
Fasten off.
To make the hat's bobble, work as for holly berry using yarn C.

07 Make up the bottle.
Weave in all loose ends. Sew Santa's 'hair' along the edge of the hat. Sew the beard, hair and hat to the centre of the label. Sew the bobble on the end of the hat, and sew two black seed beads for eyes. Make a ch with 3mm hook and yarn G long enough to fit just inside the edge of the label and sew in position. Sew the label to the bottle. With gold lurex thread, make a line of chain stitches just inside the edge of the bottle cap.

MATERIALS: CARROT

ONE 100g BALL (452m/494yd) OF SIRDAR COUNTRY STYLE 4PLY IN CLEMENTINE 541 (H), OR SIMILAR YARN (4PLY-WEIGHT ACRYLIC AND WOOL BLEND)

(OPTIONAL COLOURS FOR MAKING TWO ADDITIONAL CARROTS: 8m/9yd SKEINS OF DMC TAPESTRY YARN, TWO SKEINS IN EACH OF 7947 (I) AND 7052 (J), OR SIMILAR YARN – 4PLY-WEIGHT WOOL)

ONE 25g (70m/77yd) BALL OF HAYFIELD BONUS TOYTIME DK IN EMERALD 916 (E)

SIZE 3.5mm (US E4) CROCHET HOOK

POLYESTER TOY STUFFING

SEWING NEEDLE

HOW TO MAKE...THE CARROT

01 Make carrot for Rudolph.
With 3.5mm hook and yarn H, ch6 and ss to join into a ring.
Round 1: Ch1, 8dc into the ring, ss to the ch at beg of round to join.
Round 2: Ch1, 2dc in each dc of previous round, ss to ch at beg of round to join. 16 sts
Cont working 1dc in each st in a spiral, without closing off each round with a ss, as follows:
Ch1, 48dc (three rounds on these 16 sts).
Dc2tog, 29dc, (counts as two rounds of 15 sts where the dc2tog is 1 st).
Dc2tog, 27dc, (counts as two rounds of 14 sts where the dc2tog is 1 st).
Dc2tog, 25dc, (counts as two rounds of 13 sts where the dc2tog is 1 st).

Cont in this fashion until you have worked:
Dc2tog, 17dc.
Skip 1 st, 8dc.
Skip 1 st, 7dc.
Skip 1 st, 6dc.
Skip 1 st, 5dc.
Skip 1 st, dc2tog, break yarn and fasten off leaving long end and use to sew up end of carrot.

02 Stuff with polyester toy stuffing using the blunt end of the crochet hook to poke stuffing through the hole at the top of the carrot.

03 Optional step: Make carrots for Dancer and Dasher.
If you want to make more carrots for Santa's other little helpers, work as for Rudolph's carrot using yarns I and J.

04 Make up carrot.

Weave in all loose ends. Wind yarn E five or six times around two fingers, and pull these loops off the fingers, holding them together at one end. Use the working end of the yarn to bind these loops together tightly at one end by winding it round several times. Hold this in position firmly and cut the working end of the yarn, leaving about 20cm (8in) to use for sewing. Thread this end with a needle and sew a couple of stitches through the binding of the loops to secure them. Place the bound end of the loops inside the hole at the top of the stuffed carrot so that the binding is hidden. Sew around the base of the stalk with the tail end of yarn to attach it to the inside of the hole at the top of the carrot. Fasten off. Cut through the loops of the stalk to make individual strands of yarn.

Abbreviations

(UK terms used throughout)

beg: beginning

ch: chain

ch sp: chain space

cont: continue

dc: double crochet

dc2tog: double crochet two stitches together (decrease by one stitch): insert the hook in the first st, yarn round hook and pull it through this stitch (2 loops on hook). Insert the hook into the second st, yarn round hook and pull it through this stitch (3 loops on hook). Yarn round hook and pull through all 3 loops on hook.

magic loop and ch 1: Make a loop with the yarn around your index finger so that there are two strands at the point where the ends pass one another. Put your hook underneath these two strands and pick up the yarn (make sure you use the working end which runs to the skein rather than the tail end), pulling it under the strands so that the yarn is over the hook. Pick up the yarn again and pull it through the loop on the hook to make one chain.

rep: repeat

ss: slip stitch

st(s): stitch(es)

UK/US crochet differences:

UK dc (double crochet) = US sc (single crochet)

FUN-TO-CUSTOMISE
SHOPPING TOTE

DECORATE THE FRONT OF A PLAIN, STORE-BOUGHT TOTE BAG WITH THIS SMARTLY-DRESSED SANTA. MADE FROM FABRIC AND FELT SCRAPS, HE IS SIMPLE TO SEW. A CONTRAST LINING MAKES THE BAG REVERSIBLE SO YOU CAN USE IT ALL YEAR ROUND AND NOT JUST FOR CHRISTMAS!

GO HO, HO, HO-LIDAY SHOPPING!

HOW TO MAKE... SHOPPING TOTE

MATERIALS

PLAIN CANVAS SHOPPING BAG

SELECTION OF SMALL PIECES OF RED PATTERNED FABRICS

FELT: BLACK, WHITE AND DARK GREY

FUSIBLE WEBBING

LIGHTWEIGHT PATTERNED FABRIC FOR THE BAG LINING

EMBROIDERY THREADS: RED, WHITE, BLACK, PALE PINK AND DARK GREY

EMBELLISHMENTS: MINI METAL BUCKLE, TWO RED BUTTONS AND ONE SMALL WHITE POMPOM

SEWING THREADS TO MATCH FELT AND FABRIC COLOURS

TRACING PAPER, PENCIL AND WATER-ERASABLE FABRIC PEN

EMBROIDERY AND SEWING NEEDLES

SCISSORS

IRON

SEWING MACHINE (OPTIONAL)

SEE P93 FOR TEMPLATES

01 Copy the Santa template onto tracing paper, re-sizing it to fit the front of your bag as necessary. Slip the paper template inside the bag and trace it onto the fabric using the water-erasable fabric pen.

02 Take the template out and turn it over to the wrong side. Trace the hat, hat trim, body, belt, legs, boots, gloves, beard and moustache pieces onto fusible webbing. Iron each piece onto fabric or felt. Cut out as follows: from your selection of red patterned fabrics – hat, body and arms, and legs; from white felt – hat trim, beard and moustache; from dark grey felt – gloves and boots; from black felt – belt.

03 Peel the paper backing off each piece and arrange on the front of your bag over the relevant part of the traced outline (before placing the belt be sure to thread on the buckle). Iron into place, then stitch around the edges to secure.

04 Sew two buttons to Santa's body and a pompom bobble to his hat. Stitch over the outlines for the facial details to finish the embellishment as follows: backstitch the nose, mouth and eyes with dark grey embroidery thread, adding long stitches for the pupils; backstitch the cheeks with pink embroidery thread; and work French knots with white embroidery thread and as close together as possible for the eyebrows.

05 To make the bag lining, fold your patterned lining fabric in half. Place the bag on top, aligning the bottom edge with the fold in the lining fabric. Trim the top and side edges of the lining fabric, leaving a 1.5–2cm (⅝–¾in) seam allowance all the way around.

06 With right sides facing, stitch along each side edge to join the two layers of fabric together. Press the seams open, then fold over a hem at the top edge (front and back).

07 Place the bag lining inside your embellished bag, making sure to line up the bottom and side edges. Pin the upper hem into place just below the top edge of the bag, then slip stitch to hold the lining in place.

KIRSTY NEALE

Kirsty is a freelance writer and designer-maker. She specialises in fabric and paper projects and enjoys combining new materials with vintage or repurposed finds. Her work has been published in numerous books and magazines, and she blogs at www.kirstyneale.typepad.com

CHRISTMAS TREE

EVEN THE SMALLEST OF DWELLINGS REQUIRES A CHRISTMAS TREE. THIS ONE IS MADE FROM PRETTY JAPANESE PAPERS IN GREEN, SILVER AND GOLD AND IS VERY STRAIGHTFORWARD TO MAKE BASED ON A SIMPLE FOLDED FAN SHAPE. YOU COULD JUST AS EASILY MAKE YOURS FROM GIFTWRAP, OR GO FOR AN ALL WHITE LOOK FOR SOPHISTICATED ELEGANCE.

HOW TO MAKE... CHRISTMAS TREE

DESIGNED BY CLARE YOUNGS

MATERIALS

14 PAPER RECTANGLES, TWO OF EACH MEASURING 21 x 28cm (8¼ x 11in), 18 x 28cm (7 x 11in), 16 x 28cm (6¼ x 11in), 13.5 x 26cm (5¼ x 10⅛in), 12 x 26cm (4¾ x 10⅛in), 9 x 25cm (3½ x 9⅞in), 6 x 22cm (2⅜ x 8⅝in)

PIECE OF PATTERNED PAPER MEASURING 11.5 x 11.5cm (4½ x 4½in) FOR THE TRUNK

ONE SHEET OF A4 (US LETTER) SILVER PAPER FOR THE BASE

TWO 30cm (12in) WOODEN BARBEQUE SKEWERS

THIN WIRE

PENCIL AND RULER

CRAFT KNIFE AND CUTTING MAT

SMALL PAIR OF SCISSORS

GLUE STICK AND QUICK-DRYING GLUE TUBE

DARNING NEEDLE

01 Start by making the base for the tree. Cut strips of paper 2cm (¾in) wide. Take the first strip, run a glue stick along one side and start winding it up into a tight coil. As you come to the end of one strip, glue on another strip and continue winding, until you have a disc at least 3.5cm (1⅜in) wide. The wider the base the more stable the tree will be; to ensure your tree stands straight, make the base as flat as possible.

02 Taking one of the larger paper rectangles, place it pattern side down with one of the short edges facing you and fold over by 1.5cm (⅝in). Turn the paper over and fold the other way, again by 1.5cm (⅝in). Continue to concertina fold in this way to the end of the strip (if you are left with a spare bit that is not big enough to fold, trim it off).

03 Trim the ends of the folded strip to a point, curving the cut slightly to give a scalloped point.

04 Fold the pleated strip in half and press firmly at the crease. Run a glue stick along one edge of the fan shape and stick to the other edge to make a semi-circle.

05 Fold the correspondingly-sized paper rectangle in the same way, then stick the two semi-circles together to form a complete circle.

06 Take a small piece of wire approx 14cm (5½in) long. Fold it in half and poke the ends through at the centre of the circle from front to back on either side of the two joined semi-circles. Turn over and twist the ends of the wire together to secure. This completes a branch layer. Repeat steps 2–6 to make the other six branch layers from the pairs of paper rectangles.

07 Take the patterned paper square (for the trunk) and run the glue stick over the reverse side leaving a 2cm (¾in) strip unglued along one edge. Starting at the unglued edge, roll up to make a tube approx 1.5cm (⅝in) in diameter. Cut into sections as follows: one measuring 2.5cm (1in), three measuring 2cm (¾in) and two measuring 1.5cm (⅝in).

08 Starting with the second smallest circle, begin to thread the paper fold circles onto the skewers, placing the skewer ends through the holes where the wire joins the two semi-circles. Setting aside the two smallest paper tubes, use the paper tubes in ascending size to separate the paper fold circles. Push the circles/tubes along the length of the skewers to approx 1.5cm (⅝in) from the top.

09 Once the largest circle has been threaded on, it is time to secure the tree to the base. Prepare the base by using the darning needle to pierce two holes approx 1cm (⅜in) apart either side of the centre. Thread on one of the set-aside small paper tubes, place a blob of quick-drying glue into each hole, and push the skewers right down into the holes.

10 Thread the other small paper tube onto the skewers at the top of the tree, place a blob of quick-drying glue onto the end of each skewer and stick the smallest paper fold circle on to finish.

ROUND ROBINS

CHRISTMAS INSPIRATIONS

01

Welcome your Christmas guests with this lovely wreath design from Charlotte Lyons. Wrap a polystyrene form in colour coordinating scraps, tuck a few decorative trimmings into the folds, and fashion a little bird from felt for the centre. www.charlotte.lyons.com

02

This pretty little snowflake design is just one of six available from Polka & Bloom. Stitch them on table linens or simply leave the fabric in the embroidery hoop and add a festive ribbon for a lovely Christmas ornament. For the full range of designs see www.polkaandbloom.com and to find out more about their talented designer Carina, visit her blog at carinascraftblog.wardi.dk

03

A flock of Christmas robins, each sporting a sweet little moss stitch scarf, designed by Jooles Hill. sewsweetviolet.blogspot.co.uk

04

Large snowflake-style plates make lovely candle holders for the Christmas table. Designer Ilaria Chiaratti impressed vintage lace doilies into white modelling clay using a plate as her mould. For more great ideas from Ilaria visit her blog idainteriorlifestyle.blogspot.com

05

Bring a warm glow to your home with this great idea from Eva Gáti. Tealights are displayed in recycled shallow tins decorated with berry-red papers, and hung from a wooden hanger with decorated pegs. kiflieslevendula.blogspot.com

06

Why just wrap and tape when you can go 3D? A glue gun takes wrapping to a whole new level, and you can't fail to be inspired by Agnes Blum's extreme gift wrapping ideas.

07

Agnes Blum believes that wrapping makes the present and she shares her top five tips for decorating gifts with you at her blog knockknockingblog.blogspot.co.uk

GIFTWRAP
AND
CANDLELIGHT

POLAR PALS

FINGER PUPPETS

INSPIRED BY THE INHABITANTS OF THE NORTH AND SOUTH POLES, THESE LITTLE FELT PUPPETS MAKE FANTASTIC CHRISTMAS PRESENTS FOR KIDS. THERE ARE FIVE TO CHOOSE FROM, BUT IF YOU CAN'T BEAR TO GIVE THEM AWAY, STUFF THEM WITH COTTON WOOL TO MAKE SEASONAL DECORATIONS, AND KEEP THEM FOR YOURSELF.

SET OF
FIVE ADORABLE
CHARACTERS

HOW TO MAKE... FINGER PUPPETS

DESIGNED BY KIRSTY NEALE

MATERIALS

FELT: SMALL PIECES OF LIGHT GREY, DARK GREY, WHITE, CREAM, BLACK, TEAL, MOSS GREEN, LIGHT BROWN, DARK BROWN, RED, YELLOW, DARK PINK AND LIGHT PINK

EMBROIDERY THREADS: BLACK, WHITE, CREAM, DARK GREY, LIGHT GREY, LIGHT BROWN AND TEAL

SMALL SCRAP OF JERSEY FABRIC FOR INUIT GIRL'S SCARF

SMALL BLACK BEADS FOR EYES

SCISSORS

WATER-ERASABLE FABRIC PEN AND TAILOR'S CHALK

PVA OR FABRIC GLUE AND PAINTBRUSH

EMBROIDERY NEEDLE

PINS

TIP

Choose wool felt or a wool blend for best results. Mark your template pieces onto the felt using a water-erasable fabric pen for the lighter colours and tailor's chalk for the darker felts.

01 To make the snow fox, use the templates and a fabric pen to mark then cut out the required pieces from felt as follows: from grey felt – one upper head, one tail and two body pieces; from white felt – one lower head, one stomach and one tail tip. Also cut two shallow semi-circles from light pink felt for the cheeks and a small black felt circle for the nose.

02 Glue the stomach onto one of the body pieces and the tip onto the tail. Stick the upper head onto the lower head, then add one cheek to each side of the lower head, and the nose on the centre tip of the upper head.

03 Mark on the eyes and stitch with a single strand of black thread.

04 To create the 'fur', sew short, straight stitches randomly over the grey felt using 2–3 strands of grey embroidery thread.

05 Pin the side and top edges of the body sections together, catching in the tail at one side. Sew through all layers using a simple running stitch, removing the pins as you go.

06 Glue the head to the top of the body, tipping it at a slight angle to add extra interest and character to the finished snow fox puppet.

07 To make the Inuit girl, use the templates to cut one face from cream felt, one hood from teal felt, one sweater and two sleeves from moss green felt and two body pieces from black felt. Also cut two semi-circles from dark pink felt for her shoes and two small light pink circles for her cheeks. Make up in the same way as the snow fox, and use two beads for her eyes and a single strand of black embroidery thread for her nose and mouth. Cut scraps of jersey fabric and fringe the ends to make her scarf.

08 To make the penguin, use the templates to cut one face and one stomach from white felt, and one head, two flippers and two body pieces from dark grey felt. Also cut two shallow semi-circles from light pink felt for cheeks and two from yellow felt for feet, and a triangle of yellow felt for the nose. Sew on two bead eyes to finish.

SEE P94 FOR TEMPLATES

09 To make the polar bear, use the templates to cut one head, one snout and two body pieces from white felt. Also cut a black felt triangle for the nose and round off the edges. Sew on bead eyes and embroider the leg division and 'claws' with a single strand of black embroidery thread.

10 To make the reindeer, use the templates to cut one head and two body pieces from light brown felt, two dark brown antlers and a cream stomach. Also cut a small red circle for the nose. Embroider on the closed eyes, and stitch small horizontal running stitches on the stomach (in grey) and head (in cream).

TIP
To cover the back of your stitches and give a neater finish, glue an additional piece of felt over the back of the snow fox's head and tail pieces after you've sewn on the fur texture.

TWO TO KNIT
BERIBBONED CUSHION

THIS CO-ORDINATING CUSHION COVER AND LAVENDER SACHET FEATURE A STRIKING BUT SIMPLE TO KNIT STITCH PATTERN. MADE IN SOFT, NEUTRAL COLOURS AND FINISHED OFF WITH CONTRASTING RIBBONS, THESE ARE IDEAL PRESENTS COMPLETE WITH THEIR OWN GIFT-WRAP BOW!

CHOOSE TO KNIT BIG OR SMALL!

HOW TO MAKE... BERIBBONED CUSHION

MATERIALS: PILLOW COVER

TWO 100g BALLS (200m/219yd) OF ROWAN CREATIVE LINEN IN STRAW 622 OR SIMILAR YARN (DK-WEIGHT LINEN/COTTON BLEND)

ONE PAIR OF 5mm (US 8) KNITTING NEEDLES

TAPESTRY NEEDLE

FABRIC: APPROX 0.5m (1/2yd)

SEWING THREAD IN MATCHING COLOUR

SEWING NEEDLE

IRON

45 x 45cm (17³/₄ x 17³/₄in) CUSHION PAD

APPROX 2m (2¹/₄yd) OF NARROW RIBBON

TENSION TIP
The project features garter stitch, which is quite stretchy so tension is less important here, as long as the knitted square fits the cushion cover.

HOW TO MAKE...THE PILLOW COVER

01 Making the knitted part.
With 5mm knitting needles and holding the yarn double, cast on 55 sts.
Rows 1–10: Knit.
Rows 11–96: K8, (k1, yo, k2tog) thirteen times, k8.
Rows 97–105: Knit.
Row 106: Cast off.
Weave in loose ends. Press the piece to make it even all over.

02 To make up the cushion, start by cutting the fabric so it measures 48 x 112.5cm (19 x 44¼in) – don't worry if the length is not exact.

03 Double fold and press one short end by 2.5cm (1in) and hand-sew the hem.

04 Fold over the other short end by 45cm (17¾in) and press; now fold the hemmed end over to give you the cushion cover shape and press again. Open the fabric out and fold in each of the long sides by 1.5cm (⅝in), and press.

05 Turn the fabric over and hand-sew the knitted piece onto the cushion front (centre panel) so it sits in

place. Turn the fabric back to the wrong side, place the cushion pad in the centre panel and refold as step 4. Slip stitch the sides of the fabric together catching in a small part of the knitted piece to make it hold. To finish, wrap the ribbon around the cushion and tie in a bow.

VIBE ULRIK SONDERGAARD

Danish knit designer Vibe Ulrik Sondergaard studied fashion design and photography. She currently works as a designer, producing hand-knitted swatches that are sold to fashion companies in New York, LA, Paris, Barcelona and London. Vibe's colourful, textured designs are both practical and beautiful.

MATERIALS: LAVENDER SACHET

ONE 50g BALL (130m/142yd) OF ROWAN PIMA COTTON DK IN LOZENGE 055 OR SIMILAR YARN (DK-WEIGHT 100% PIMA COTTON)

ONE PAIR OF 3mm (US 2/3) KNITTING NEEDLES

TAPESTRY NEEDLE

15 x 30cm (6 x 12in) PIECE OF FABRIC

SEWING NEEDLE

DRIED LAVENDER

APPROX 40cm (16in) OF NARROW RIBBON

TIP
The distinctive stitch pattern is made by teaming together an increase, made by a yarnover (yo) with a decrease (k2tog).

HOW TO MAKE...THE LAVENDER SACHET

01 Make front part of sachet.
Using 3mm knitting needles,
cast on 25 sts.
Rows 1–10: Knit.
Rows 11–44: K5, (k1, yo, k2tog)
five times, k5.
Rows 45–53: Knit.
Row 54: Cast off.

02 Make back part of sachet.
Using 3mm knitting needles,
cast on 25 sts.
Rows 1–53: Knit.
Row 54: Cast off.

03 Weave in loose ends. Press the
piece to make it even all over.

04 To make up the lavender sachet,
put the front and back knitted
pieces together, wrong sides
together, and sew three of
the seams.

05 Fold the fabric in half and sew
two sides together to make
a pocket. Turn the 'pocket' inside out
to hide the seams and fill with
dried lavender. Sew together the
final seam and put the flower-stuffed
bag into the knitted sachet.

THE LAVENDER SACHET MEASURES 13 x 13cm (5 x 5in)

06 Sew the last seam of the knitted
sachet closed. Weave in any loose
yarn ends. Finally, wrap the ribbon
around the sachet and tie in a bow.

Abbreviations

(UK terms used throughout)
k: knit
k2tog: knit two stitches together
(decrease by one stitch)
st(s): stitch(es)
yo: yarnover

MACHINE-EMBROIDERED
CHRISTMAS PICTURE

FREEHAND MACHINE EMBROIDERY IS A GREAT WAY TO CREATE A FESTIVE PICTURE. SIMPLY PLACE YOUR MOTIFS ON A BACKGROUND FABRIC AND USE YOUR MACHINE NEEDLE AS YOU WOULD A PEN TO CREATE REALLY INTERESTING STITCHED DETAILS. YOU WILL NEED TO LOWER THE FEED DOGS ON YOUR MACHINE AND USE A DARNING/EMBROIDERY FOOT.

CREATIVE CHRISTMAS COLLAGE

HOW TO MAKE... CHRISTMAS PICTURE

SEE P93 FOR TEMPLATES

MATERIALS

TWO PIECES OF CONTRASTING FABRIC FOR THE BACKGROUND: APPROX 23 x 48CM (9 x 19IN) FOR 'GROUND' AND 27CM x 48CM (10½ x 19IN) FOR 'SKY'

APPROX 35 x 46CM (14 x 18IN) WADDING (BATTING)

FABRIC SCRAPS OF YOUR CHOOSING FOR THE PICTURE MOTIFS

SEWING THREADS: RED, BROWN AND YELLOW

FABRIC SPRAY ADHESIVE

23CM (9IN) EMBROIDERY HOOP

WATER-ERASABLE FABRIC PEN

SEWING MACHINE

DARNING/EMBROIDERY FOOT

FABRIC SCISSORS AND SMALL EMBROIDERY SCISSORS

01 Pin the two pieces of background fabric together horizontally, with right sides facing, to make a square piece of fabric. The 'sky' area will make up the top two-thirds of the piece and the 'ground' the bottom third.

02 Machine stitch using a 1.5cm (⅝in) seam. Press open the seam, turn over to the right side and press the piece well along the seam line.

03 Cut a piece of wadding to the same size as the background and pin to the wrong side of the fabric. Fix the fabric in the hoop: place the inner hoop under the background fabric on the wrong side and the outer hoop over the top of the inner hoop on the right side, ensuring that there is a little more 'sky' than 'ground'; attach with the top screw piece. Remove any pins from inside the hoop.

04 Enlarge the picture templates and cut out of paper. Pin the templates to the wrong sides of your chosen fabric scraps, and cut out ensuring that the shapes will be facing the right way once placed with right sides facing on the background fabric.

05 Spray the back (wrong side) of each picture piece with spray

fabric adhesive. Place in position with right sides facing up on the background fabric.

06 Using a darning/embroidery foot on your sewing machine and with the feed dogs in the down position, freehand machine embroider the motifs, using two lines to outline each piece with red sewing thread.

07 Continue to add the detail to the picture: use brown thread for the reindeer's eye and collar, and the reins leading to the sleigh; use red thread for the reindeer's nose. Embroider red and yellow baubles on the trees and red bows on the parcels. Trim the loose ends of thread at the front and back of the work after sewing each piece.

08 When all the picture pieces are stitched in place, trim the edges of the background fabric allowing approx 5–10cm (2–4in) from the edge of the hoop. Add a loop for hanging.

TIP

If possible use a Perspex foot so you can see through it to the fabric. Keep the needle in the automatic stop down position, so if you need to take a stitching break the needle won't go off track.

NICKI TRENCH

Nicki Trench is dedicated to the revival and promotion of home crafts. She is a prolific writer of craft books as well as lecturing and feature writing on patchwork, quilting, crochet, sewing, knitting, hen keeping and vegetable gardening. To find out more see www.nickitrench.com or visit her blog nickitrench.blogspot.co.uk

PAPER DECORATION
STRING OF STARS

MADE FROM PATTERNED PAPER, RECYCLED BOOKS AND A HINT OF SEASONAL SPARKLE, THESE PRETTY STAR GARLANDS OFFER A FUN ALTERNATIVE TO TRADITIONAL TINSEL OR PAPER-CHAINS. STRING THEM ACROSS A ROOM, A WINDOW, OR BETWEEN THE BRANCHES OF THE CHRISTMAS TREE TO ADD SOME STELLAR STYLE TO YOUR HOLIDAY DÉCOR.

HOW TO MAKE... STRING OF STARS

MATERIALS

PATTERNED PAPER

OLD BOOKS

METALLIC OR GLITTER PAPER

WHITE SEWING THREAD

PENCIL

SCISSORS

SEWING MACHINE

TIP
Look out for paper that is printed or coloured on both sides so that your finished stars are beautiful from all angles. To save time, you could use a star punch or star-shaped die and die-cutter as an alternative to hand-cutting your stars.

01 Make a star template from cardboard and use to draw around this onto your chosen papers.

02 Bundle the stars together in groups of six. Alternate between the different types of paper and mix up the colours too.

03 Pull out a long length of bobbin and top thread from your sewing machine (this will make it easier to hang up your garland when you have finished). Align the edges of your first star bundle, then feed it through the machine, sewing along the centre through all six layers.

04 When you reach the top, keep sewing for a few centimetres (couple of inches) with nothing under the foot, then add your second star bundle. Stitch along the centre as before.

TIP
You'll find it easier to sew through the paper bundles if you start at the base and stitch towards the top point of the star. Change your needle afterwards as sewing on paper will blunt it.

05 Keep going, adding one bundle of stars at a time and leaving a small amount of 'blank' thread in between. You can make these gaps an even size or vary them if you prefer.

06 When you're happy with the length of the garland, stop stitching and pull out another long length of thread as you did at the start. Snip the ends to release.

07 Finally, fold the layers of each star bundle gently along the stitched centre line so that they splay outwards to create a pretty, dimensional paper star.

DESIGNED BY KIRSTY NEALE

SEE P95 FOR TEMPLATE

01

02

03

04

05

SIMPLY STITCHED
CUTE CHARACTER NAPKINS

DRESS UP SIMPLE CLOTH NAPKINS FOR CHRISTMAS WITH THESE SWEET LITTLE CELEBRATORY MOTIFS HAND-EMBROIDERED ONTO BRIGHT FABRIC CIRCLES. CHOOSE A DIFFERENT COLOUR CIRCLE FOR EACH, SO YOUR GUESTS CAN KEEP TRACK OF THEIR NAPKIN THROUGHOUT THE FESTIVE DINNER.

HOW TO MAKE... CUTE CHARACTER NAPKINS

MATERIALS: PER NAPKIN

ONE PIECE OF BRIGHTLY-COLOURED COTTON FABRIC MEASURING 13 x 13CM (5 x 5IN)

EMBROIDERY THREADS: WHITE AND COLOURS TO MATCH YOUR FABRICS

CLOTH NAPKIN

WHITE SEWING THREAD

WATER-ERASABLE FABRIC PEN

EMBROIDERY HOOP

EMBROIDERY NEEDLE

SCISSORS

PINS

IRON

01 Trace your chosen motif onto the brightly-coloured fabric. Place the fabric in the embroidery hoop to keep it nice and taut as you stitch.

02 Using white embroidery thread, embroider the design using six strands for the main outlines and three strands for the smaller details. Use a backstitch for the outlines and mouths, and French knots for the eyes and berries (on the pudding).

03 Remove the embroidered fabric from the hoop and trim to a 9cm (3½in) diameter circle, making sure that the embroidery is centred in the circle.

04 Cut a 7cm (2¾in) diameter circle from paper and place in the centre on the back of the embroidered fabric circle; pin in place. Stitch a large running stitch around the edge of the fabric.

05 Pull the thread to gather the edges in around the paper circle template. Tie off the thread, then press. Remove the template.

DESIGNED BY MOLLIE JOHANSON

06 Pin the fabric circle to the corner of the napkin. With six strands of matching coloured embroidery thread, sew a small running stitch around the edge of the circle to secure it to the napkin.

07 With three strands of coloured embroidery thread, sew a running stitch border around the edge of the napkin, stitching along the hem and only catching the top layer.

TIP
By embroidering onto circles of fabric not only do you identify each person's napkin, but you also keep your stitches hidden from view. You could add matching circle motifs along the edge of the tablecloth too.

SEE P95
FOR
TEMPLATES

Running stitch

Backstitch

French knot: bring needle up at 1, wrap thread around needle twice, then down at 2, holding thread taut around needle while pulling through the fabric.

EASY FAIR ISLE
FINGERLESS GLOVES

THESE FINGERLESS GLOVES ARE JUST WHAT YOU NEED TO KEEP WINTERTIME CHILLS AT BAY. THE INTRICATE FAIR ISLE DESIGN ON THE BACKS OF THE GLOVES IS AN ATTRACTIVE TAKE ON TRADITIONAL PATTERNS, WHILE THE RIBBED SECTIONS AT THE PALMS HELP GIVE THEM A SNUG FIT.

KEEP WARM
AND COSY

HOW TO MAKE... FINGERLESS GLOVES

TENSION TIP

26 sts and 38 rows to 10cm (4in) square over st st using 3.25mm needles. Finished size laid flat: approx 9 x 20.5cm (3½ x 8in) after washing and sewing up.

MATERIALS

50g BALLS (225m/246yd) OF THE WOOL SHED ALBAYARN, ONE EACH IN SUMMER PUDDING (A), TEAL (B), LICHEN (C), LOCHAN (D), SPRING (E), MOSS (F) AND WINTER WHITE (G) OR SIMILAR YARN (4PLY-WEIGHT WOOL)

ONE PAIR OF 3mm (US 2/3) AND ONE PAIR OF 3.25mm (US 3) KNITTING NEEDLES

TAPESTRY NEEDLE AND GLASS-HEADED PINS

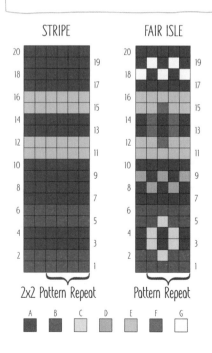

STRIPE   FAIR ISLE

2x2 Pattern Repeat   Pattern Repeat

A B C D E F G

01 Reading the Fair Isle chart.
The back of the gloves features a Fair Isle design. Use two colours at the same time across a row, following the colour sequence from the chart below left. Each square represents a stitch; each horizontal line a row. Read the chart from the bottom right corner: knit or right-side rows run from right to left; purl or wrong-side rows from left to right. The design features a 20-row pattern repeat that is knitted twice, then the first 6 rows are repeated again (46 Fair Isle rows in all).

02 Understanding the pattern.
The gloves are knitted flat, then seamed together. The cuffs are knitted in a 2x2 rib. Once the cuff is complete, work the section that forms the back of the glove, including the Fair Isle panel, in st st, while continuing the palm in rib. The thumbs are made in rev st st.
The Fair Isle design for the right glove is worked at beginning of the row; for the left glove, it comes at the end of the row. When working a Fair Isle pattern you hold two colour yarns at the same time; simply 'float' or carry the colour not in use across the back of the row. This design is worked so you do not have to carry the colour over more than 3 sts.

03 Make the right glove from the cuff.
Using 3mm needles and yarn A, cast on 54 sts (see stripe chart).

Row 1: K2, *p2, k2, rep from * to end.
Row 2: P2, *k2, p2, rep from * to end.
These 2 rows form the 2x2 rib pattern; rep the last 2 rows a further 8 times (18 rows in total).

04 Knit the main part of the right glove.
Change to 3.25mm needles.
Row 1 (RS): K2, *p2, k2, rep from * 5 more times, M1, k to end of row. 55 sts
Row 2 (WS): P31, k2, *p2, k2, rep from * to end.
Carry on working 26 sts in 2x2 rib, working stripes as set out on the stripe chart, while the 29 sts of the st st section sets up the Fair Isle panel (see Fair Isle/FI chart).
Change to yarn B but do not break off yarn A.
Row 3 (RS): K2, *p2, k2, rep from * 5 more times, work row 1 by working in knit to the end of the row.
Row 4 (WS): Work as follows:
Join in yarn C at beg of this row to keep the fabric even. Insert RHN into first st purlwise, then bring up yarn C and place it across yarn B.
Next, work the first 2 sts as you would normally. The contrast yarn should now be caught behind the main colour. Drop yarn B, pick up yarn C and work the next st as FI chart, then cont in this way until all the sts on the chart have been worked.

Complete the row using yarn B as follows: p2, *k2, p2, rep from * to end.
Cont working 2x2 rib pattern and working from FI chart as set until row 13, using colours below for rib section.

Rows 5–6: Yarn A.
Rows 7–8: Yarn B.
Rows 9–12: Yarn A.

05 Place the thumb.
Join in yarn E but do not break off A. On the next row, start to increase for the thumb using M1: pick up the strand between sts by inserting your RHN from the back to the front of the strand, then insert your LHN from the back to the front under this loop and slip over onto the LHN, then purl as usual.

Row 13: K2, *p2, k2, rep from * 4 more times, p1, M1, p1, k2, work row 11 of FI chart. 56 sts
Row 14: Work row 12 from FI chart, p2, k3, p2 *k2, p2, rep from * to end (work rib in yarn A).
Row 15: K2, *p2, k2, rep from * 4 more times, p1, M1, p1, M1, p1, k2, work row 13 of FI chart. 58 sts
Row 16: Work row 14 from FI chart, p2, k5, p2, *k2, p2, rep from * to end (work rib in yarn E).
Row 17: K2, *p2, k2, rep from * 4 more times, p1, M1, p3, M1, p1, k2, work row 15 of FI chart. 60 sts
Row 18: Work row 16 from FI chart, p2, k7, p2, *k2, p2, rep from * to end.
Row 19: K2, *p2, k2, rep from * 4 more times, p1, M1, p5, M1, p1, k2, work row 17 of FI chart. 62 sts
Row 20: Work row 18 from FI chart,

p2, k9, p2, *k2, p2, rep from * to end (work rib in yarn A).
Row 21: K2, *p2, k2, rep from * 4 more times, p1, M1, p7, M1, p1, k2, work row 19 of FI chart. 64 sts
Row 22: Work row 20 from FI chart, p2, k11, p2, *k2, p2, rep from * to end (work rib in yarn B).
Row 23: K2, *p2, k2, rep from * 4 more times, p1, M1, p9, M1, p1, k2, work row 1 of FI chart. 66 sts
Row 24: Work row 2 from FI chart, p2, k13, p2, *k2, p2, rep from * to end (work rib in yarn A).
Row 25: K2, *p2, k2, rep from * 4 more times, p1, M1, p11, M1, p1, k2, work row 3 of FI chart. 68 sts
Row 26: Work row 4 from FI chart, p2, k15, p2, *k2, p2, rep from * to end (work rib in yarn B).
Row 27: K2, *p2, k2, rep from * 4 more times, p1, M1, p13, M1, p1, k2, work row 5 of FI chart. 70 sts
Row 28: Work row 6 from FI chart, p2, k17, p2, *k2, p2, rep from * to end (work rib and thumb in yarn A).
Row 29: K2, *p2, k2, rep from * 4 more times, p16, turn.
Next row (WS): K15 – work on these 15 sts only to create thumb.
Work a further 11 rows in rev st st.
Cast off knitwise.
Break off yarn, leaving length of yarn and use to sew down thumb seam until you reach yarn B.

06 Continue glove as follows.
With RS facing and using yarn A, pick up 2 sts at base of thumb, k2, then work

row 7 from FI chart. 57 sts
Row 30: Work row 8 from FI chart, p2, k4, *p2, k2, rep from * to end of row.
Row 31: K2, *p2, k2, rep from * 4 more times, (p2tog) twice, k2, work row 9 from FI chart. 55 sts
Row 32: Work row 10 from chart, p2, *k2, p2, rep from * to end.
Keep working 2x2 rib at beg of row and the Fair Isle patt as set on rem 29 sts until a further 16 rows have been completed.
Change to 3mm needles.
Break off yarn B and use yarn A for the next 3 rows and the cast-off.
Next row: K2, *p2, k2, rep from * 5 more times, k2tog, knit to end. 54 sts
Next row: K30, p2, *k2, p2, rep from * to end.
Next row: K2, *p2, k2, rep from * 5 more times, knit to end.
Cast off in rib for 26 sts, then cast off knitwise to end.

Abbreviations

(UK terms used throughout)
beg: beginning
k: knit
LHN: left-hand needle
M1: make 1 (increase by one stitch)
p: purl
rem: remaining
rep: repeat
rev st st: reverse stocking stitch
RHN: right-hand needle
st(s): stitch(es)
st st: stocking stitch

07 Make the left glove.

Work as right glove until cuff completed. Work main part of glove as follows:

Row 1: K28, M1, k2, *p2, k2, rep from * to end. 56 sts

Row 2: P2 *k2, p2, rep from * 5 times, p to end.

Join in yarn B but do not break off A.

Row 3: Work row 1 of FI chart, k2, *p2, k2, rep from * to end.

Row 4: P2, *k2, p2, rep from * 5 times, work from row 2 of chart.

Cont working in patt from the FI chart and 2x2 rib as set until row 13, using colours indicated below for rib section.

Rows 5–6: Yarn A.

Rows 7–8: Yarn B.

Rows 9–12: Yarn A.

Work rib in yarn E.

Row 13: Work row 11 of FI chart, k2, p1, M1, p1, k2, *p2, k2, rep from * 5 more times. 56 sts

Row 14: P2, *k2, p2, rep from * 4 more times, k3, p2, work row 12 from FI chart (work rib in yarn A).

Row 15: Work row 13 of FI chart, k2, p1, M1, p1, M1, p1, k2, *p2, k2, rep from * 5 more times. 58 sts

Row 16: P2, *k2, p2, rep from * 4 more times, k5, p2, work row 14 from FI chart (work rib in yarn E).

Row 17: Work row 15 of FI chart, k2, p1, M1, p3, M1, p1, k2, *p2, k2, rep from * 5 more times. 60 sts

Row 18: P2, *k2, p2, rep from * 4 more times, k7, p2, work row 16 from FI chart (work rib in yarn A).

Row 19: Work row 17 of FI chart, k2, p1, M1, p5, M1, p1, k2, *p2, k2, rep from * 5 more times. 62 sts

Row 20: P2, *k2, p2, rep from * 4 more times, k9, p2, work row 18 from FI chart.

Row 21: Work row 19 of FI chart, k2, p1, M1, p7, M1, p1, k2, *p2, k2, rep from * 5 more times. 64 sts

Row 22: P2, *k2, p2, rep from * 4 more times, k11, p2, work row 20 from FI chart (work rib in yarn B).

Row 23: Work row 1 of FI chart, k2, p1, M1, p9, M1, p1, k2, *p2, k2, rep from * 5 more times. 66 sts

Row 24: P2, *k2, p2, rep from * 4 more times, k13, p2, work row 2 from chart (work rib in yarn A).

Row 25: Work row 3 of FI chart, k2, p1, M1, p11, M1, p1, k2, *p2, k2, rep from * 5 more times. 68 sts

Row 26: P2, *k2, p2, rep from * 4 more times, k15, p2, work row 4 from chart (work rib in yarn B).

Row 27: Work row 5 of FI chart, k2, p1, M1, p13, M1, p1, k2, *p2, k2, rep from * 5 more times. 70 sts

Row 28: P2, *k2, p2, rep from * 4 more times, k17, p2, work row 6 from FI chart.

Row 29: Work row 7 FI chart, p16, turn.

Next row (WS): K15 – work on these 15 sts only to create thumb.

Work a further 11 rows in rev st st.

Cast off knitwise.

Break off yarn, leaving length of yarn and use to sew down thumb seam until you reach yarn B.

08 Continue glove as follows.

With RS facing and using yarn A, pick up 2 sts at base of thumb, p1, k2, *p2, k2, rep from * to end. 57 sts

Row 30: P2, *k2, p2, rep from * 4 more times, k4, p2, work row 8 from chart (work rib in yarn E).

Row 31: Work row 9 from FI chart, k2, (p2tog) twice, k2, *p2, k2, rep from * to end. 55sts

Row 32: P2, *k2, p2, rep from * 5 more times, work row 10 from FI chart (work rib in yarn A).

Keep working Fair Isle patt as set on 29 sts at beg of row then 2x2 rib until a further 16 rows are completed.

Change to 3mm needles.

Break off yarn B and use yarn A for the next 3 rows and the cast-off.

Next row: K27, k2tog, k2, *p2, k2, rep from * to end of row. 54 sts

Next row: P2, *k2, p2, rep from * 5 times, knit to end.

Next row: K30, *p2, k2, rep from * to end.

Cast off 30 sts knitwise, then cast off rem sts in rib as set.

09 Finishing off and making up.

Wash in tepid water, then squeeze out water gently. Place gloves on a padded surface; pin out Fair Isle section only to block and leave to dry. Weave in loose yarn ends and sew up the side seams.

TEMPLATES

ALL THE SHAPES FOR THE BOOK'S MAKES. ENLARGE ALL TEMPLATES BY 200% BY PHOTOCOPYING THE PAGES, WITH THE EXCEPTION OF THE HEIRLOOM STOCKING WHICH SHOULD BE ENLARGED BY 400%. YOU CAN ALSO FIND THE FULL-SIZE TEMPLATES READY TO DOWNLOAD FROM WWW.LOVECRAFTS.CO.UK

PAPER CUT ORNAMENT

Horse

Stand

—— Cut

---- Fold

– – Score

SHOPPING TOTE

CHRISTMAS PICTURE

FINGER PUPPETS

All Finger Puppets Body

Snow Fox Upper Head

Penguin Head

Snow Fox Lower Head

Penguin Face

Snow Fox Stomach

Snow Fox Tail

Penguin Stomach

Snow Fox Tail Tip

Penguin Flipper

Inuit Girl Face

Reindeer Antler

Inuit Girl Head

Inuit Girl Sleeve

Inuit Girl Sweater

Reindeer Head

Polar Bear Head

Polar Bear Snout

Reindeer Stomach

BAUBLE GIFT BAGS

Gift Bag

cut opening on one side

place on fold

FESTIVE STATIONERY

DOOR WREATH

STRING OF STARS

HEIRLOOM STOCKING

Bauble

Collar

Nose

Ears

Eye

Deer

Oval

IPAD COSY

NOTE: THE HEIRLOOM STOCKING
TEMPLATES NEED ENLARGING BY 400%.

Main Stocking
(A)

Stocking Top (B)

Toe (C)

Heel (D)

CUTE CHARACTER NAPKINS

PUBLISHER'S ACKNOWLEDGMENTS

This book would not have been possible without the input of all our crafty contibutors. We would also like to thank Cheryl Brown, who has done a brilliant job of pulling everything together, and Sophie Martin for her design work. Thanks also to Leah at KraftyChicDesigns (www.etsy.com).
Project photography by Rachael Smith, as follows: p7, 11, 13, 21, 25, 29, 35, 39, 43, 47, 51, 59, 63, 69, 73, 77, 81, 85, 89.
And of course, thanks must go to the fantastic team at Mollie Makes for all their help, in particular Jane Toft and Kerry Lawrence.

For more information on Mollie Makes please visit www.molliemakes.com

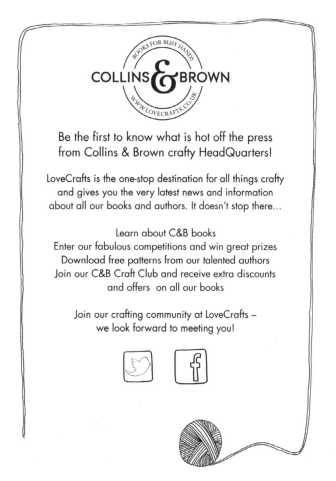

COLLINS & BROWN

BOOKS FOR BUSY HANDS
WWW.LOVECRAFTS.CO.UK

Be the first to know what is hot off the press from Collins & Brown crafty HeadQuarters!

LoveCrafts is the one-stop destination for all things crafty and gives you the very latest news and information about all our books and authors. It doesn't stop there...

Learn about C&B books
Enter our fabulous competitions and win great prizes
Download free patterns from our talented authors
Join our C&B Craft Club and receive extra discounts and offers on all our books

Join our crafting community at LoveCrafts – we look forward to meeting you!

First published in the United Kingdom in 2012 by
Collins & Brown
10 Southcombe Street
London
W14 0RA

An imprint of Anova Books Company Ltd

ISBN 978-1-90844-917-7

A CIP catalogue record for this book is available from the British Library.

10 9 8 7 6 5 4 3 2

Reproduction by Mission Productions Ltd, Hong Kong
Printed and bound by G. Canale & C. S.p.A. Italy

This book can be ordered direct from the publisher at
www.anovabooks.com